TIGER MOTHER
SON OF A BITCH

TIGER MOTHER
SON OF A BITCH

THE STORY OF HOW THE ADULT SON OF A TIGER MOTHER

THINKS ABOUT HIS MOTHER'S PARENTING AND THE

EFFECTS THAT IT HAD ON HIM

by

DERRICK LIN

Cover & Text Design by: Vince Pannullo
Print by: RJ Communication.

Printed in the United States of America

ISBN: 978-0-578-07893-9

DEDICATE

I would like to dedicate this book to my father, Chinese people, Korean people, Japanese people, and in fact all people who have to suffer the same dilemma that I went through. I hope this book can let others understand what goes on behind the supposedly rosy success stories and how these people who suffer really feel. Yeah!

CONTENTS

Introduction..9

Chapter 2: What I went through 11
Chapter 3: Motherfucking plastic assembling type toy with
    different colors 15
Chapter 4: My mother 17
Chapter 5: College life 23
Chapter 6: When I was a child 31
Chapter 7: The other person who I was abused with 37
Chapter 8: Humor 45
Chapter 9: Hungry..51
Chapter 10: Some relief but not much 63
Chapter 11: A new start 67
Chapter 12: I can't take this shit anymore..........................71
Chapter 13: My new extended family..................................79
Chapter 14: My interests and past time hobbies 87
Chapter 15: Good times in China 93
Chapter 16: Good times in the US.....................................99
Chapter 17: More hobbies...103

My thoughts...109

Introduction

HELLO there my name is Derrick. I think my mother sucks balls. You see dear reader, it is a result of the way she raised me. She is what you might call a "Tiger Mother". She is such a bitch. I think that she can go fuck herself. During the past few years my life has been a living hell. I have attempted suicide two times and seen several psychologists one of whom I flipped out on because of her insistence on me using antidepressants. I dropped out of college because I was working two jobs and could not pay my tuition. At the time that I am writing this, I should be looking forward to graduating in the spring. I was supposed to at least finish my undergraduate studies but I am nowhere near that objective. Why? I am supposed to be successful. I am Chinese American. I was born and raised in the US. I learned the piano, violin, trumpet, and drums because I was forced to. I practiced for countless hours under my relentless mother and was forced to join an orchestra on Wednesdays and perform recitals that I hated. I was forced to go to Chinese school on Saturdays and do all my homework correctly at the threat of not being allowed to sleep in the house. I wasn't allowed to have friends. Shouldn't I be overachieving like my other Asian cohorts? The answer is Fuck Yeah I SHOULD, but I'm not. I was thoroughly prepared for it by an overbearing mother. She forced me to do things that no other child my age was doing. Why haven't I succeeded? Instead I am working at a donut shop for minimum wage and I haven't been in school for nearly three years. I hate my mother. Well I can't say hate since its such a strong word but how about strongly dislike. In fact the only reason I haven't kicked her ass is because she is my mother. Every time when I see her I refuse to talk to her. When I do talk to her I usually make a lewd gesture or use obscene language to deliberately upset her. I tell my colleagues and friends about how I dislike her. Even as I write this now I feel like throwing up at the thought of my mother. She sucks, she really does. She will live a long life unfortunately. Its in her genes. Therefore I have no choice but to suffer continuously.

CHAPTER 2

WHAT I WENT THROUGH

WHEN I was younger, I didn't think in this manner. In fact, I listened to everything my mother said and told me to do. Like many Chinese children, I submitted willingly because my mother told me that it was Chinese culture and respect. I did her laundry as well as mine when I was seven years old. I cleaned the house, and threw out the garbage. I did chores. Sounds harmless right? WRONG!!!! Right now I am still doing all these fucking chores for her and I'm twenty one. She keeps telling me that its good training for me and that I have to learn. I think she is a piece of shit. She can burn in hell for each time she says something senseless like that. Every time I drive her somewhere I have to open the door for her and use my hand to lift her out of the car. I know about courtesy and manners but she's not a fucking invalid! I don't understand why I have to do everything for her such as hammering nails in the wall so that she can put up pictures of herself all over the walls. I keep telling her that its pointless since we don't even have company over much but she says, "NO RESPECT!" and threatens to make me sleep outside. I used to be scared at that and then I would always do what she told me to do. However now I simply say, "suck my cock", (not literally of course) and she has the nerve to get upset!! I can't believe it, what more does this insane bitch want?!!

I remember hearing from my relatives that when I was born, the physician who delivered me knew what the deal was when he talked with my mother. I can't imagine what happened but I can certainly think about it. My mother told me that when I was born I was measured very long and the physician said, "This boy is going to be at least six feet tall, at the least", thus starting my nightmare. To this day I think about my height and why I did not reach six feet although I keep telling myself that height has nothing to do with a person's worth. So my fucking mother has been telling me since I was born that I am supposed to be tall and shit like that. I do not know what her goddamn fascination is with me being tall but you can already see where this is going.

I will get back to that story later but for now, hmm… lets see… oh yes! I remember now. Well actually I don't but my dad and aunt told me so that should be good enough. So after my mother gave birth to me my parents took me home. We didn't live in New York long since my father thought that such a place was not conducive to raising a child and we moved to New Jersey. My father knew my mother was lazy as fuck so he hired a babysitter to take care of me since my mother "had no strength" according to her own words.

When I was four years old I will never forget what lesson my mother first taught me. She taught about me about money and its use as a tool. She laid out some bills on the floor and forced me to add them up to varying sums. Pray tell me why you ask? To make me aware of modern society? So that I could do simple math? So that I could know the value of a dollar? She taught me about the value of money, so that I could make money in the future and give it to her. That's right! Give it to her, for safekeeping of course but I knew it sounded like bullshit at the time already.

So after this informative lesson of how I owed her everything because I was her son, she then told me that anyone who turned on a light must turn it off. I mean the light switch of course but at the time I was pretty confused about the money thing since she didn't let me sleep until 1AM that day until I was able to make and give change accurately so that I didn't lose any of her precious money. Earlier she had turned on the light in the living room where the money lesson was taking place (I saw her do it) and now she went to the bedroom to sleep. I yelled after her that she should turn off the light since she herself turned it on. However my mother then told ME to turn it off. I was dumbfounded. Hadn't this bitch just taught me the lesson that whoever turns the light on has to turn it off?

So I screamed at her to turn it off and she naturally refused saying that I had to learn and undergo life training. I thought to myself that she could go to hell but I grudgingly turned off the light switch after several minutes of arguing and screaming. I will always remember that incident as I am telling you now. So then the next day, my mother starts to teach me math and reading. She keeps saying how important it is for me to do math and reading. Again she teaches me for several hours until I get it right and I'm crying and screaming at her because I only want to go to sleep since it wasn't until 2AM by the time I finished.

So this was how I was raised. It was supposed to be all rosy and ideal but in the end as you can tell, it fucking wasn't. Not even slightly. I feel like jumping off a building anytime I am forced to do something she tells me to. For instance repairing my motherfucking toy thing that I hated structures. I don't mean to bash this toy thing, I think its very nice and a great invention. It stimulates children and blah blah blah. When you ask a twenty one year old to do this shit, that is when it becomes overbearing! That's what my mother tells me to do. She mentions it whenever she can, "Derrick you have to do this because its about respect and its bad feng shui if you don't" and of course I'm thinking that she's a compete psychopath and I just ignore her.

CHAPTER 3

MOTHERFUCKING PLASTIC ASSEMBLING TYPE TOY WITH DIFFERENT COLORS

WHEN I was nine years old I built the thing. It was a type of product that kids would assemble, not like building blocks but there were many plastic pieces that could be assembled. The final assembled thing would resemble a model of a building. Let's call this thing motherfucking toy thing that I hated. I think it was some sort of factory or whatever the thing said. Anyway I built the thing and it took me three weeks. At the time I think its safe to say a nine year old would probably find this project to be challenging. I built it and I was proud of my achievement. The damn thing was taller than me. I had a right to have pride in it. It was one of my biggest regrets.

Every summer until I was eleven years old I had to build a different motherfucking toy thing and I immediately hated the second one. I cried and screamed at my mother explaining that I didn't want to do it but she threatened me if I didn't by saying that I would have to pay rent or sleep outside on the street. So I had no choice but to build them. Now I understand when a parent wants a child to go through on his or her word. I understand the concept of making an effort. I think in this case my mother went too fucking far. She kept saying how important it was for me to learn about engineering and shit. I told her that I didn't want to do anything that she forced me to do since they weren't in any way conducive to making a living. But she forced me and I went fucking crazy starting from that incident.

Those motherfucking toy thing that I hated structures weren't designed for durability. At least not after eleven years. We would later move at least two times and I can tell you that they were a pain in the ass. They were tall and cumbersome to say the least. The first time that we moved, I asked my mother to throw them out. They were too much of a burden as I thought then and now. She refused. She said that it was her motherfucking toy thing and if I did she would simply order another box for me to build. I remember crying and screaming at her to throw them out but she simply refused. In fact, she threatened me with the prospect of sleeping outside if I did anything to damage them. She would regret that decision later on.

I think anybody should be able to start seeing a pattern here. My mother's overbearing personality and her mentality would be factored into every aspect of life. Whether it was going on vacation, going to the mall, or buying groceries I would suffer at her hands somehow.

CHAPTER 4

MY MOTHER

PERHAPS I should elaborate upon my mother's background. Yeah that should clarify something about her right? So from what I gathered, in her youth my mother was not very talkative. She was also hated by her parents because she was a female. Oh right, let me explain this. In Chinese society men come first and women come second or sometimes not at all. What I'm trying to say is that Chinese culture is mainly patriarchal and men are generally regarded as more important because they can do manual work, retain the family name, and have children to keep the family in existence. This goes back ancient Chinese culture where some asshole named Confucius decided that was how people should behave. I say asshole because he completely obliterated the concept of masculinity or machoness, something that I admire and note is lacking from many Chinese males, but this isn't a story on why I can't get laid so I won't bother about that here (maybe you would like to hear about THAT story someday).

Anyhow my mother was not looked upon favorably by her parents because she was wasn't a man. Sounds kind of unfair if you ask me but whatever, I'm no goddamn civil rights activist but it might have had a profound impact on my mother and why she enjoys abusing other people for her pleasure. I'm being serious, I think she genuinely enjoys it, that's how she gets off. Whatever, but it sucks for the one who is taking the abuse.

I have met that side of the family. Her family lives in Taiwan and I had the chance to visit and live with them for a couple of weeks. Some of her family lives in Thailand but that point is irrelevant. Why don't I give you my perception of my mother's family. Long story short, they suck. I had never seen such uptight people in my life. I am beginning to think that its in my mother's genes to be such an asshole. Her parents for one didn't treat her well. They treated me like shit when I went there. My grandfather would give me a suspicious look every now and then go to womanize. My grandmother would do the same thing, only she sat in the house and did not womanize. My cousins were quite distant to me as well with the exception of one who had been educated in an international school. She was very nice and I feel sorry for her since I need to talk shit about the rest of her family but what I say is the truth. Her father, my uncle, was also quite nice, and I suppose her brothers and mother were too. Other than that, I disliked them all. I felt uncomfortable there so now when I go and visit them, I just take the money they give me and leave immediately.

Back to my story, I can remember my awareness of the situation when I graduated high school and started college. It was only at that period of time that I began to question her authority. As a child if she made mistakes, I did not have the capability to realize how wrong she was, but I did at this stage. So I go into a state college and I thought that I would build my future there. I had aspired to become a doctor and as a result I wanted to do the medical program there and eventually intern at the hospital nearby which was linked to the program. I chose the state university not for its good academics, or football team but rather the mere fact that it was the closest and cheapest. I couldn't afford any other college being that they were out of the budget for me. So I had to go there and commute to class everyday since I only had enough money saved for one years worth of commuting to school.

I had given thought as to where I was going to get the money once my first year was over. This money was the accumulation of all the birthday parties, summer jobs, and holidays on which I received gifts of cash. I didn't mind spending my own money to build myself a future but initially I thought my mother was going to pay for it since that was the plan and the way most Chinese or any caring family would do for their children. My father had once told me that a college degree was very important and I sought not to let him down. He told me that I should get a bachelor's degree at the minimum for my own benefit. I respect him for that. As for my mother however, she had other plans.

I will tell you why my mother did not pay for my college tuition. She didn't have the money to do so. Initially my father left me more than enough money to get me an undergraduate degree. My mother lost it all through mismanagement and never told me. In fact I only figured it out recently. I couldn't get student loans because my mother had no income and could not cosign a loan for me. I could not get federal loans because my mother owned a piece of real estate and it exceeded the minimal amount of assets that would have allowed me to qualify for federal loans. This fact only exacerbated my hatred for her.

My mother didn't tell me about this aspect. She told me she was not going to pay for my college tuition because I should learn the value of a dollar. I was supposed to work, get a job, and go to school without any help from her at all. At the time I felt mildly pressured about this, but now I am angry at about this in particular. That's how much of a "Tiger mother" she is. She will let her only child suffer and fail despite having had the resources to do otherwise. My mother should have had the college funds ready for me rather than mismanage it.

When I use the term mismanage, I have to explicate the context on which it was mismanaged. My father had left us money when he divorced my mother. It was more than enough for me to go to school and not have to work at the same time. The money was supposed to be enough if my mother had gotten a job and produced income. The money should have been invested in some safe investment vehicle. Apparently my mother was too lazy to work so instead we had to live off of that money for several years. So we ate into our egg money. The principal should have never been touched. Now I know what happened to my college fund.

I know it is good to push your children. What doesn't kill you will only make you stronger. But I felt that this was inexcusable because my father purposely left me money to go to school without having to work. Its really not fair for her to push and abuse me all my life to prepare me for something that I can't do. My college should have been paid for. But it wasn't. I suffered all the way up until I was seventeen just to hear her say to me, "you need to take out loans for college". It was bullshit. I feel like beating the shit out of my mother for that alone but I can't, because she is my mother.

CHAPTER 5

COLLEGE LIFE

I began to get the feeling that she wasn't so enthusiastic about me going to college as she was in me making money and then giving her money. Even though she would not be paying for my college, I still felt up to the task of working and studying at the same time. I kept stressing that I would be making tons of dough after graduating and making my living as a high flying doctor. At that point I took on two jobs to pay for the costly tuition to come. Then she started to tell me what classes that I should take and how many credits that I should take. Now I don't know if its normal to take more than twelve credits a semester. I guess I'm just a wimp but I thought that twenty would be somewhat excessive. She wanted me to take that many so I could complete college quicker, make money, and then give it to her faster. I was always wrong since I was an inexperienced child according to her so I ended up taking about sixteen credits per semester.

I can still remember being on the phone with my mother, handing it over to my academic counselor, and saying to her that my mother wanted to speak to her about choosing my courses. I shudder at that memory and my naiveté at that period of time.

I was about seventeen years old at the time and up until then I had willingly submitted to my mother's words of wisdom since I had no outside sources to compare them against. All my life I had to listen to her, do what she told me to do despite the fact that I hated doing whatever it was that she told me to do. Now I realize that she had been enslaving and torturing me all those years. I should have kicked her ass. Or at least called social services.

Anyhow college opened my eyes. Not so much my contact with other people my age but rather the fact that real life was starting to sink in. As I mentioned before, I didn't have much money for more than my freshman year of study so I decided to get a job. No, in fact I got two jobs. One working as an electronics salesperson and another as a telemarketer selling car warranties. I had to study for all the prerequisites for pre-med also so it was quite hard. In fact soon I was going to class late everyday since I had to work full time, study, and commute two hours everyday to school. Little did I know that this period of hardship would liberate me.

Liberate me from what? From being hard working and making an effort? Finally getting a chance to party and have a social life? No. I finally was able to repudiate my mother. I snapped. I started to completely ignore her. Well it didn't happen overnight. Or maybe it did. I remember how it started but there were factors that culminated in that act.

I was going to my chemistry class (which was hard as fuck) and I remember thinking that if I could pull off all B's in my courses then I would definitely stick it out. I poured my heart and soul into studying and working. When I got to class the professor was handing out the grades from the latest exams. I thought that I had done decent on the recent exams at the time because I had put a lot of effort into studying despite my full time job. I even went to study sessions and learning centers to enhance my comprehension of the schoolwork. I was wrong.

The professor was handing out the grades on pieces of paper. Everyone in the room was cringing when they saw their grades. I scoffed and thought confidently that my arduous childhood had prepared me for this very moment. Those hours of torture that my mother forced me to practice math, English, and piano should finally pay off. I turned the paper over that the professor gave me and looked at it. I got a D.

At first I thought I was just too tired and that it was a B. Then I suddenly snapped out the trance I had been in for those months of nonstop working and studying and I looked more carefully. It wasn't a B, it was a D. My heart sank and I crumbled at that very moment. But I was free.

Shit didn't matter anymore. Nothing did. All my mother's teachings had in fact been shit. Wow I thought. Damn. Oh well. Of course I was in denial. It wouldn't be until a few months later that I completely freed myself from the clutches of my mother. So I went home and slept. The next day I went back to school and didn't go to class. I just sat on a bench and thought. At that time my mother was in China on a business trip doing some real estate thing and I was home alone. Then I decided that I wasn't worthy enough and started to think about committing suicide.

I had failed. No A. No B. Not even a C. A D. I started to write my suicide note and thought of the ways that I could commit suicide. I thought about hanging myself but then decided against it. I thought about crashing my car into a tree. Hmm that might not do the job. Finally I felt that it would be best if I jumped off a building. That way I should most definitely be dead. I didn't realize it but I was starting to do things just to spite my mother. I could finally get back at her. All her hard effort in raising and torturing me, down the drain. That would be the ultimate slap in the face.

Of course I didn't realize that was what my intention was. That I wanted to simply repay my mother for the years of suffering that she caused me. Or that I was now free. I really thought I should commit suicide because I wasn't good enough. Because I wasn't Asian enough. I had let down all my Asian peers in my inability to succeed academically. I felt worthless. Therefore I had no right to live and take up others space.

But even then I had doubts about suicide. I was depressed but inside of me I thought that there was something weird about it. I actually felt happy for the first time in my life. Knowing that my suicide would cause my mother pain. So I called the suicide hotline being unsure of what I should do. Of course my erratic behavior was noticed by others on campus and I guess I didn't even have to call the suicide hotline since some nice student decided to do it for me. Wow, Americans sure are considerate.

So the police came because they were all scared about me. Well not scared but pretty concerned since at the time school shootings were on the rise. I matched the description, Asian, male, suicidal, so they came right away. They interviewed me and everything and forced me to see a psychologist. I went. It only made things worse.

I remember going to see the school psychologist and I was thinking to myself, " I wonder how these people are going to help me?", and anticipating something wonderful. So the psychologist saw me, lets call her Marcy. Marcy had dark hair and a confidence that only a degree and certificate can provide and she started to ask me questions. I explained that I was Asian and that it was a travesty that I should even get such a low grade. I told her about how my mother raised me and forced me to study math, English, and any other schoolwork for hours to the point where I only slept six hours a day for six days a week for most of my life up to that point. I explained to her that I was frustrated about my low but passing grades in Biology, Chemistry and Math.

Marcy told me that the transition to college was hard on everyone and that it wasn't my fault. So I thought to myself, "Wow I'm starting to feel better already", and then Marcy told me to take some prescription antidepressants. Then I said, "suck my cock", and I left.

So after several lewd gestures to my groin and slamming the door at that particular psychological counseling office I decided that I was hungry. I went to a fast food restaurant that I frequented and then I sat down to eat. As I was eating, I saw an advertisement for some university help line. I forgot the name of this organization but it was like a hotline where people could call and rant their frustrations. I decided to do just that. After all what harm could it do? Certainly better than talking to some bitch psychologist. Right? WRONG!!!!!!!!!

I drove home and I called the number and started to talk. I got some girl on the line and we chatted about stuff. Then I started to talk about the recent events surrounding me and the girl got scared. Lets just say that the conversation didn't end so well. The girl then got frightened or something because I was talking about how I had just tried to kill myself. What a wimp! Anyhow my mother was nearby (oh shit....) and heard the conversation. The girl on the phone was asking me for my address and said that it was for my own safety. My mother immediately refused and she snatched the phone from me and pressed the button on it to end the call.

So about ten minutes later the police showed up at my door and took me to the hospital. My mother was screaming and balking but I went knowing that at least she was frightened now. At the hospital I was examined by a psychologist there and he said that in the end that I was a perfectly sane individual. He told me that my major problem was my mother and that I should get the hell away from her, in fact the further the better. Aha! Now you see where the final revelation took place.

After that I was finally free. I no longer had to listen to my mother. In fact that was the beginning of my liberation. I was about eighteen years old and I broke free of my mother's hold on me. I started to not do her laundry, only use her grocery money for my portion of groceries, and refuse to drive her anywhere. I would not do shit for her. I vented all my anger on her. She had set me up to fail.

I think I was a little more relieved at this point because I didn't care about my mother anymore. I remember being enraged at her for no reason. There was this one time I saw her in the kitchen and I began throwing things and breaking them. I broke a window and punched a few glasses. I threw a chair around. Now I could actually vent all the anger I had accumulated during my childhood. My mother was scared. I was happy to see that.

I think I should elaborate more about my childhood. I should let you see the bigger picture as to why I turned out this way. Now all I do is think about is to make a living, nothing more. I don't want to be a doctor, or a real estate agent like my mother was forcing me to do. (Yeah by the way my mother is a real estate broker, I'll tell you more about how that affected me) I just want to be happy. Much better right? Well, I can never obtain that dream until I get away from my mother. As I am writing this, I am sadly living with her now. But it's a lot better because I just ignore her all the time 24/7. I still cringe though.

CHAPTER 6

WHEN I WAS A CHILD

MY childhood was fairly normal. I suppose if you factor in the beatings, the threats, and the forced labor it was quite normal. I liked watching cartoons. So my mother forbade me to watch TV. Ever. She would hit me with the remote control if I did. Also no candy, cookies, pudding, pizza, hamburgers, or any food that made life pleasurable. I was forced to only eat vegetables and meat. However I could drink juice so that was good. Prune juice. I liked computer games. So she took them away and threatened that I would sleep in the garage and the in scary dark if I tried to play them. What else? You know, dictatorship type stuff.

So apart from that I guess I was pretty normal. My mother didn't let me have sleepovers or play with friends. She allowed me to have friends but not to have playtime with them. What a fucking bitch. Maybe that's why I have such bad social skills now when it comes to leisurely pursuits. I had to learn to do the laundry when I was seven. I had to iron the clothes and fold them. My mother's clothes as well. I disliked that. And throw out the garbage and clean the floors. It doesn't sound so bad when you think about it but she also expects me to do it now as a grown adult. Do you see where I'm going with this?

I know that children should respect their parents. Its only natural. But I don't think they should if their parents don't respect them. You haven't lived the life, don't pass judgment yet. Wait until I'm done. Then you can give your opinion. So what was I saying? Oh yeah my childhood.

Did you ever play an instrument? Ever play in a band? Did you like it? I hated it. Not because I don't like music. I was forced to play it. I was forced to play the piano, violin, trumpet, and drums. It was a nightmare. I hated going to music lessons, I hated playing in recitals, I hated it all. So when I was about five, my mother decided to force me to play the piano. Now when I say force I mean force. Some kids might play the piano for a while and then decide that they don't like it. They then switch to some other activity and go their merry way. I couldn't. I don't mean I didn't want to, I MEAN I could not.

My mother threatened me that if I didn't play the piano I would have to sleep outside, in the dark. I was deathly afraid of the dark and more so of sleeping outside. She made it seem like it was the end of the world or her way. I had no choice. I screamed and cried every time she brought me to the music center. I tried to hide underneath the pianos. I tried to walk very slowly to the room. I was forced to play the piano.

When I was home my mother forced me to practice the piano everyday. Fortunately she didn't emphasize the importance of music. Rather she said that music was important in my development. So that's a sigh of relief. At least I didn't have to practice for hours on end. Then she bought a violin for me.

"What the fuck is this orange looking thing?", I mused. Apparently my mother wanted to add this instrument to my piano playing. I initially thought it was interesting and a fun looking instrument. I didn't know how wrong I was. Fortunately for me I found out very quickly as I went to my first violin lesson. I remember my teacher teaching me about the violin for about thirty seconds and I hated it already. I didn't like it. I already thought the piano sucked (because I was forced to play it) and now this shit.

I personally have no disrespect for anyone who enjoys the violin, piano, or any other instrument. In fact I rather enjoy such instruments myself when I listen to music. I just hate doing things that I don't want to do. So I was tortured for about six years playing both the piano and violin. Even though I only had to practice half an hour for each a day, I had to now practice two instruments so it was an hour. I would throw tantrums each time I went to school to play the instruments. It got me nowhere. When I got home my mother would give me a beating and force me to kneel down in a dark room for an hour. I was scared shitless and I cried frequently, mainly because I was afraid of the dark which she knew I was of course.

Therefore I had to endure the piano and violin lessons. Then my mother decided to join the local orchestra. Pure terror I tell you. So now I had to practice one hour for my lessons and practice another half hour for the orchestra everyday. Bullshit. And you thought that half an hour was easy. That's what makes my mother suck, she will give you something mildly annoying or tortuous but then compound it with more mild requests. Soon you're being tortured full on without even realizing it until its too late.

So the orchestra sucked. I have nothing against them. I was forced to join against my will. I hated it. Every Wednesday for two fucking hours we would get together and practice. My mother would also play the violin to make things worse. Oh that made things a lot worse. I was forced to practice while my mother lazed around and did nothing. What a bitch. Then the orchestra would give recitals and concerts. Oh that really sucked ass.

I'll tell you more about the musical horrors later. Now I would like to introduce you to the concept of Chinese school. What's so special about that you may ask? Well let me tell you. Chinese school takes place on Saturdays. In fact it takes place between nine in the morning and twelve in the afternoon. Not so bad right? After all I should keep up with my own heritage. Okay I am somewhat grateful for the Chinese school. I can speak Chinese fluently now as a result of those years of hard study.

I have nothing against Chinese school or those who attend. I think its wonderful that people are embracing the fact that China is an emerging power and blah blah blah. But seeing my classmates stay home on the weekends and sleep in made me feel that it was unfair. My mother worsened the experience by beating me and threatening to make me kneel in a dark room if I didn't get good grades. She forced me to study all Saturday afternoon and review on Sunday. Wow what a life I had.

When I mean forced, I mean that I had to write a Chinese characters perhaps ten times. No fifty times. No a thousand times. Or as much as it took for me to remember that word. My mother told me that I should be thankful because many children grow up on farms and have to milk the cows at four in the morning. As if that's relevant to my life. She told me that I was spoiled and that she never had such a privileged life when she was young. I told her to fuck off and then she spanked me. So back to the writing. If I couldn't do my homework properly or prepare well enough to get a hundred on a Chinese test, I would be beaten. It was because my mother would lose face amongst the Chinese community for not teaching me.

That's kind of selfish if you think about it. But my mother lived on pride. She was like a prim Donna. Goddamn bitch. She twisted things to her own benefit. She deliberately lied to me just for her own advancement. She wanted to show off her glorious child to others so that they could compliment her. What a cunt.

This pattern would go on and in fact still goes on. But enough about that for now. I remember though Chinese school started to become less important when my mother became a real estate agent. She started to harass people at the Chinese school to let her sell their houses for them. Once her name became soured she stopped forcing me to do the homework. I started to get fourteens and fives on tests. I didn't do any of my Chinese homework. Actually her name soured everywhere and the burden was relieved on me. My grades dropped even in normal school.

I was actually experiencing a time of freedom and joy. But it didn't last long. That was about the last year of middle school for me. Then I went to high school. Now there was more emphasis than ever for me to do well in school because I had to go to college. My mother forced me once again to do my schoolwork well. She said it was necessary for me to go to college so that I could make more money and give more to her. However this time she didn't force me as much as she did before.

Chapter 7

The other person who I was abused with

I think I know why. You know what? I have barely talked about my father. Why don't I do a little of that? My father is a role model to me. I look up to him. He talks about having principle. Just imagine him as a ideal man with intelligence, kindness, and generosity to match. We were both tortured by my mother. I asked him why he married her. He mentioned to me that when he married her he could never imagine that she was so terrible. He had just been discharged from the military in Taiwan and had little prospects. He felt honored that any woman would go with him given his low status. Eventually when he immigrated to the US and immigrated my mother, he began to regret his decision.

He had to work two jobs constantly. My mother would stay at home and do nothing. That basically characterizes the relationship. She wouldn't cook, clean, or work to make a living. I don't know how my father tolerated it as long as he did but I think his training in the special forces for ten years helped. He worked hard for a better future. My mother contributed nothing and sat at home doing nothing. This isn't just hearsay from my father. All my relatives say the same thing about her. They said that she was lazy and couldn't do anything. Maybe this is why she forced me to do everything. She wanted to make another slave after my father divorced her.

Oh yeah I forgot to tell you, my father eventually got tired of the bullshit with my mother not working and being lazy and constantly complaining. Before I was forced to do all the house-work, my father did it. So my father divorced her after some twenty years of marriage. He was greatly relieved by the divorce. Good stuff. I think the melting point for my father was after he had a triple bypass surgery. He had heart disease and decided at that point to retire in China. Therefore as the person who made all the money, now we were cut off.

Now I know what you're thinking right? You're thinking, "Wow what kind of father is that?", but allow me to retort. My father knew that my mother was a useless piece of shit but did love me and knew that if my mother went down I would go down as well. By this point in time he really didn't care about my mother anymore, after all living with her was nothing but trouble. Imagine forcing a grown adult to do all your chores for you and be the main source of income. I think few people would tolerate such a thing. Let me describe this in depth before I go on about what my father did to ensure that I didn't starve.

My father worked in New York and we were living in New Jersey. On the weekdays my father would work and live there because quite frankly he knew that being around my mother was hazardous to his mental and physical health. So I only got to see him on the weekends. I don't blame him at all, in fact it would be what I would do if I had a bitch wife like. Jeez. Anyhow when my father would come home on the weekends, he would usually be exhausted from the commute and he would only spent one night there since he would drive back the next day to prepare to work.

My mother, from the moment my father stepped in the door would start to bombard him with a list of things to do, such as house repairs or hammering nails on the wall to hang up more of her portraits (She has dozens of pictures of herself). Sometimes she would even force him to go shopping for useless shit like bed covers or whatever funny object that women usually like. I don't know. But what was particularly bad about this habit was that she would not make any sense at all. Now I know women may not exhibit the same thought patterns that men might. But here I am talking about some serious deficiency in sense.

For instance I remember one time we went shopping for mattress covers. Sounds harmless right? So my mother wants some type of cover for her mattress that is made of silk or something like that. She finally finds one suitable to her insane mind and picks it out. My father buys it, and we go home to put them on the bed. So of course the cover is too small for her "Queen" sized bed. My mother did not even bother to measure them despite planning for it the day before. Hmmm. Well I know humans make mistakes right? Right? This is nothing to blame someone for. WRONG!!!!!!!!!!

Now that I have told this little parable, lets go to another one that will give you a sense of what's going on. My father owned a little business in New York, and his business needed a certain product. This day was particularly busy so he wrong down the exact product that he needed as asked my mother to receive it from a location. So my mother went to this place without writing down the exact product and decided that it would be befitting for her, since she considers herself a prodigy in business, art, and any other possible ego boosting thing that she can pick out whatever she want from the warehouse and that it will fit in perfectly. Uh-oh.

So she brings the invoice back to my father who had no time to check it carefully and the shipment comes. The product is completely wrong and my father's business for the year had no income as a result of having a backlog of useless merchandise that was not sellable resulting from my mother's decision that her idea was better. Then he had a series of heart attacks, probably from the stress, and had the open heart surgery.

To get back to where I was going with this story, here is the point I was trying to make. Imagine if my mother made a decision and applied it to everything aspect of life. From buying a harmless set of clothes to filling out an insurance claim. Yeah. Now you see where I'm going with this. But fortunately that didn't happen often because my father was around to prevent her stupidity from jeopardizing us. But now like I mentioned earlier, he was leaving us. Oh shit.

At this point in time, my father leaves the family and goes to retire (somewhere far away so that my mother will never know where he is) and my mother is bitching all the way because she knows that she can't do shit. My father is caring so he leaves my mother a decent sum of money. I don't know how much but it supposedly should be enough for 4 years of college tuition and a bit more. Now this is when I am around twelve years old. That's nice right? Sure. So now my mother is in charge of this decent amount of money. A recipe for disaster.

My mother had gotten her real estate license several years before and was trying to sell houses or whatever she was doing at the office. My father probably left her the money thinking that she would have a source of income and wisely invest the money. He slaved and saved that money for over twenty years hoping that I would have a better future. His intent was for her to make the money work for us. Hence the money would have been more than enough for my college tuition and other expenses. Of course my mother did not make any consistent income from then until now. Ah, shit.

Anyhow that's why she started being more lax with me in regards to schoolwork after I entered high school. Because now she needed to make money and train me to take my father's place. She forced me to go on the weekends when she worked in the real estate office and had me memorize and learn about the business. She brought me to conventions, to business meetings, and had me do her tasks for her. I think my mother shifted from forcing me to do schoolwork and other things that supposedly makes a child good in the line of Chinese culture to try to turn me in to a cash cow for her.

I don't know if you have realized by now but perhaps I haven't given enough information about my mother's credentials. They are quite impressive from a distance as my mother has dozens of certificates. She is a licensed beautician or some shit like that, a former court reporter, a mortgage broker, a real estate broker, and feng shui consultant. She has all these diplomas and certificates on the wall. She owns her own brokerage agency now. Sounds great right? Sounds like she can make some good money and support me or at least herself right? Wrong.

I am not sure what it is with my mother but she can't make money. Not that she doesn't know how but that she doesn't. I have yet to see any income from her in the past few years with the exception of a few real estate deals. She is so goddamned lazy, she stays at home all day and does nothing. But that's right now. I'm talking about when I was in high school.

So she's a real estate agent and she is taking me along on her job and it sucks. Instead of not having Saturdays because of Chinese school, now I have to sacrifice Saturday and Sunday because real estate usually takes place any day of the week. By the way I never got paid for any of the work I did. I am forced to plant real estate signs for her, assemble refrigerator magnets for her real estate promotion, and sit in a house while she tries to show it as an open house. As you can tell, I didn't have much of a childhood.

My mother can't make money. I think its because she is too lazy. She can't work for anybody because she won't listen to them and won't put in the effort. I know this because I have to do the work for her. She doesn't cook, clean, buy the groceries, or do the laundry. Instead she made and makes me do it now. I am so used to doing them that now I don't complain anymore. However there is a difference. Now I only do my own laundry.

This is all horrible but of course it gets worse. Since now my father has divorced her and is living as far away as he can my mother looks upon me to do things for her egotistical ass. By now I can do the schoolwork on my own and I am mature enough to do so as my father had emphasized for me to go to college. That aside, now my mother decides that I need more life skills such as putting nails in the wall so that she can hang up all her portraits. Or putting mirrors on the wall so that there are good vibes. Or putting up curtains for her so just because she likes them. Fucking bitch.

Now begins the phase where my mother just finds random things to abuse me with. Before I suppose I benefited from being forced to study or learn about certain things. However now its just ridiculous. My mother is bossing me around just to satisfy her ego. She keeps telling me however that I need to learn about life and how I am inexperienced. Yeah right.

CHAPTER 8

HUMOR

HOW about a funny story. There are actually certain moments in my life where I was able to very temporarily break free from the stress I had from my overbearing mother. This usually occurred when I did something that upset my mother but it was one of those things that was in a grey area. What I mean is that it is debatable as to whether it is right or not. When I was about five years old I remember walking on the street with my parents in the city. We were on the sidewalk and were going to a restaurant and I was walking in front of them. I don't know how I was walking but all of a sudden my mother grabbed me and told me to stand still. She said that she saw that I was walking like a gay person would.

Now I had no idea what she really meant until much later. She told me to walk with my back straight and so that my ass didn't swing around. She said that I was walking in a bad way. So fine I thought I'll walk the way she tells me to. No big deal, easy stuff to correct. Years later when I was eighteen and not caring about college, I was with some friends. I met these friends at my telemarketing job. In fact I met one guy there and he showed me his other friends. Anyhow, we got to know each other better and he invited me to several of his parties and taught me the ways of which I never knew because I was so attached to my mother until recently.

I was quite happy that someone could be so kind to consider me in that manner since I had very poor social skills due to my isolation from others when I was young as a result of being tortured by my mother. So you could say that we got to be friends. One day this friend, lets call him Mike, was near my apartment where I lived with my mother. He was with another one of his friends and he wanted to come over and see where I lived. I had already seen his home so I thought it would be nothing unusual for me to do same as he had done for me.

So these two strangers to my mother but not to me come to my house. I welcome them in and show them around. My mother happens to be there and sees them. Remember the aforementioned incident when I was five? Apparently that was not an isolated incident. My mother was and still is apparently homophobic and completely horrified at the prospect that her son might be a homosexual. So she thought these two strangers in the house were my sex partners. Hilarious right? No, it gets even better. So I realize this at that moment and I try to lead her on. I start talking about how long I have know the two friends and how we always get involved in orgies or whatever so as to scare her.

Evidently it worked quite well because my mother was silent and had a shocked look upon her face. She went quietly into her room and locked the door. I could not and still can not help laughing about this even today. The frosting on the cake was when after my friends left I confronted my mother and she started to talk about how she didn't appreciate me bringing strangers into the house. She then said that having sex with men was very dirty and I would get AIDS if I did. I tried not to laugh, but I failed. Still hilarious even now.

I enjoy a deprecating and macabre sense of humor if you have not caught on by now. I suppose it came from my inescapable suffering at the hands of my mother. I had to cope somehow, and humor became of the mediums of which I could momentarily forget my woes with some humor. There was however one thing that I never liked about myself when I was younger and I managed to change it for the better. When I was young, I was overweight and not very athletic. Due to my mother's overbearing nature and focus on academics, I did not have the chance to participate in after school sports or concentrate on physical fitness.

I did not like being fat but I did not have time to start caring for my physical health until shortly after my father divorced my mother. I was roughly around twelve years old when I started to exercise and at that time I began trying to lose weight. I had gone to China every summer to visit my father and one particular summer I gained a lot of weight. I did not realize it until I came back from China significantly heavier. I was surprised at this because I had lost weight during my summer vacations in China the previous two years at this point and I thought I had lost some more weight this time.

The past two years I spent my summer vacation in China, I lost weight because my father had rented an apartment there on the eighth floor. This building had no elevator and as a result we had to walk up and down the stairs at least three times a day. Why you ask? Why not just stay there and come out once a week? My father and I always ate out, that is why. Factor three meals a day and there you have it, a daily fat burning activity. Sometimes my father would forget his wallet and we would have to climb all the way back up the eight floors after this realization on the bottom floor. It was good for our health. But we were human and so my father finally rented a place with an elevator.

This particular year where I gained about fifteen pounds in two months, there was a sale, a daily discount at a fast food restaurant there. So we ate at this fast food restaurant for lunch everyday and sometimes even for breakfast, but we ate regular meals during dinner. Usually. That was how I became fat. At my heaviest I weighed about 184 pounds being five feet nine inches. I was obviously upset at this so I decided to start exercising with an increased intensity when I got back to the United States.

It took me over five years to lose the weight and get to where I was satisfied. As of now I am about 157 pounds and five feet eleven or ten inches. That is quite an accomplishment. I found jogging to be of the greatest help and I was eventually running three miles a day at my peak. I ran according to a system developed by an air force doctor. There were a certain amount of points that one would accumulate per distance of cardiovascular exercise. It was also timed. I think that the goal for a healthy person was to get at least thirty points per week.

Not too hard. I did about forty to sixty a week at peak times to lose weight.

I also tried dieting but none of them ever worked for me. Those fad diets only made things worse. I had tried low carb diets, low fat diets, low sodium diets, but I just could not stop masturbating. Actually to tell you the truth I still can't stop masturbating. I just get this urge inside me whenever I see women wearing high heels. I think I have a psychological problem. I usually have to masturbate nearly everyday. I had communicated this to my mother and that was part of the reason why she had brought me to see a psychologist. I'm just kidding. She brought me there because of the femdom pornography I was masturbating to, not the fact that I was masturbating. But really, I could not and still can not stop masturbating. I get so deprived without it. I remember traveling for several days without masturbating and when I finally got the chance to do so, I cummed so hard my cum hit the window five feet away from me. And I was sitting on the floor.

CHAPTER 9

HUNGRY

SINCE I am talking about sexual themes, want to hear about my mother's sex life? Sure you do. I am involved in her sex life strangely enough. When I mean involved however, I mean that my mother was so cheap she almost wouldn't give me money for anything other than groceries which were actually for her. So I usually went with my mother on her dates so that I could eat. When I mean "eat", I probably should explain the context to you. My mother is quite petite, at around four feet eleven inches. She doesn't require as much food as I do. I am almost five foot eleven and I think anyone would realize that I require more calories than my mother does in a day.

It wasn't so bad when I was younger because my mother gave me portions of food appropriate for her size and at the time, I was about her height as well. However when I grew older, she never adjusted my rations in proportion to the needs of my caloric intake. Therefore I usually went hungry since she only gave me enough grocery money for two people her size. What a fucking bitch. Thank god for public school lunches.

Back to my mother's dating. If you had a boyfriend or

girlfriend, would you expect them to pay for your child if you had one? I mean if you got together for a long time and became close I guess you would. What about if you met them for the first time?

I remember the first time my mother was dating. She had met this guy on some online dating website. I was happy to go because it meant talking to anyone other than my mother so I went. I remember the look of surprise on his face when my mother introduced us. I remember how his jaw dropped too. Needless to say, that guy lasted only one day with my mother. So on to the next guy.

This time my mother is actually wise enough to realize that bringing a child, especially a hungry one on a first date might not be so optimal for the occasion. Thankfully due to her calculated decision she decides that I should stay home and that she should request this guy to pay for a separate takeout order for me. So this guy lasts two days before he probably decided that this insane bitch wasn't worth the effort.

The third guy, lets call him Rick, actually thought that my mother was worth it. I guess Asian women are exotic in a sense in the United States and he was willing to put in the effort for that alone. I feel sorry for him. He had no idea what he was up against.

Rick from my recollection was a musician of sorts and great guy. In fact I thought he was really nice. He had a good personality, was caring, and humorous. I wished that he didn't have to suffer so much. I think my mother realized that no matter how much she tried to turn me into a cash cow at this point in time, I was just too young to do anything. So she wanted to find a substitute in the absence of my income producing father and me. Enter Jeff.

I don't mean to make out that Rick was a sucker. I mean to say blatantly that my mother simply tries to take as much as she can from other people. Even from her own son. Maybe it was her feeling that she lacked things as a child or something like that. Maybe her own inadequacy. Whatever it was it sucks for other people that she meets. I think if a reality show was made and its plot was to put my mother, and three other men on a small island, they would all commit suicide before the end of the season. She really gets to people, and from what I can tell that's one of her talents, to annoy and traumatize other people.

So this Rick guy is nice and he's taking my mother (and me) out to places, to meals, and to general points of interest. I guess he thought that all these transgressions that my mother was acting up upon were simply her PMS and that it would all go away after they got to know each other better. He was wrong. I tried to warn him but it didn't take. But then again, who would believe it? Even as I am writing this you might think I am a disrespectful son, and a menace for even saying such a thing. If you gave me the benefit of the doubt you would know better.

I shall describe some of the experiences that increasingly made Rick aware of the fact that he was not dealing with an ordinary woman. My mother has a weak stomach and is very sensitive to acidic foods. I mean like citrus fruits, vinaigrette, and foods that usually cause indigestion. So you can imagine what happens whenever she goes to a restaurant and she mistakenly orders anything that is acidic to her. I know a lot of people have heartburn and indigestion, I'm not criticizing that. What I am criticizing is the fact that my mother will always forget to tell the waiter that they should put the acidic dressing on the side or simply order food that is acidic in nature. If I got a dollar for every time she innocently forgot I could buy a new car by now. No, two new cars. Eh maybe one cheap one, sorry I miscalculated, but you know where I'm getting at right?

Then another famous demand (not request) of hers is that she needs seltzer and Cranbury juice mixed together in a martini glass. She says its because of her weak hands but I think its because she wants to show off her nonexistent classiness with a martini glass. I would hate to be the waiting staff at whatever restaurant she goes to!

Rick was nice guy. Funny too. He was an artist. He had every quality that a good partner should have. But he couldn't handle my mother. My father could do so for over twenty or thirty years because he had been in the special forces before. Rick had no chance I'm afraid. At the time I didn't realize it but I feel sympathy for him and the others who tried. It takes more than a mere mortal to deal with my mother. Fortunately this took some pressure off of me because now she left me alone.

At this period of my life I was around fourteen or fifteen so it was better but it would get bad during my freshman year of college. However I guess this was one of those times where my life was fairly tolerable because my mother had a new person to torture. Quite frankly speaking I think they were with her only because she was having sex with them. Well better than nothing but I guess this form of prostituting isn't as bad. At least I could eat more food.

It was nice having someone else for my mother to abuse. Her attention was now divided and she did not bring me to real estate conventions, or open houses as much anymore. I was also allowed to quit Chinese school. I had mentioned that I was forced to play the piano and violin, but by this stage I had switched to the trumpet and drums. They were much easier and I didn't have to practice much. Soon, I stopped the music lessons altogether. It was great. I finally had a chance to relax. Though at this point I was preparing to apply to colleges it was significantly easier because it was nothing new. I would still do all the household chores, grocery shopping, and occasionally be forced to go to a real estate seminar. However my mother's attention was now preoccupied by Rick.

I remember the many melting points where I saw Rick start to crumble. Maybe it was the fact that my mother was dating several men at one time. I don't know. I was usually involved because I was hungry and they had food in their refrigerators. I went on dates with my mother in order to eat and not starve. I mentioned earlier that she would only give me enough grocery money for two people her size. Therefore I was usually around to hear the arguments that they had with each other. They were quite amusing for me but not for my mother's boyfriends. I feel pity for them.

One thing that my mother says is "no respect!", whenever

she doesn't get something that she wants. What a pain in the ass. She is like a child who keeps whining. Of course I couldn't and still can't do anything about this annoying behavior because I came out of her womb. That's the only reason why I put up with this bullshit. Because I'm her son. What am I supposed to do? Get another mother? That's what she tells me. That she is my mother. That's why I have to respect her. You can see how this mere fact alone makes me insane.

So there was this one time when we were going out to the movies with Rick and we were at a department store after. My mother is being herself and is taking a couple of hours just to look at some useless things that she will never use. So then she sees these nine dollar dresses that are on sale. She wants them but we had just gotten out the movies and the mall was closing. Rick tells her that she can get them the next time and that he has to get back home. Sounds reasonable right? WRONG!!!!!!!!!

Now my mother just flips out and starts crying and whining about how Rick is showing her no respect and how I suck. She is screaming and crying and this is in public, at a mall you know, and Rick is just trying to make light of the situation. Then by this time, the mall is set to be closed and those dresses can't be bought because the store with the stupid fucking ten dollar, no nine dollar fucking dresses is closing. So my mother breaks up with Rick. Dinner and a movie all paid by Rick which included my portion, and my mother breaks up with Rick because of some nine dollar dresses. Ridiculous.

I didn't know at the time how come my mother was so willing break up with him but now I do. My mother had other boyfriends including one named Ben at the time. I had no idea until Ben walked in the front door the following week and introduced himself. I was thinking to myself, "Where's Rick?", but my mother told me to shut the hell up or else she wouldn't bring me back any food. So I did. Ben was a pretty nice guy too. Not as fun but he was more formal. He was an engineer and had his own house. He was also divorced and had some children. My mother liked him because he made more money than Rick. You all know where this is going.

Ben treated me well too and I had several interesting conversations with him as well. What I especially like about Ben, was the food. I might be selfish in your eyes but I was fucking starving. When I said my mother only gave me enough for two people, I REALLY mean for two people HER size. The caloric intake of 2000 calories a day prescribed by the International Red Cross was nowhere near what I was ingesting. Even with school lunches, how about the weekends? Huh? What about the fucking weekends? Am I to survive on air? Should I filter feed?

So I was quite happy with Ben as well because he sometimes brought over food. My mother doesn't cook by the way. In fact she never cooks. There was a period of time where I had to cook for her. What a bitch. Anyhow I was placated by my mother's new boyfriend. Only this time things got a bit feisty. Ben was more aware of my mother's personality in the beginning and began to suspect that things were what she said they were. Maybe it was his own paranoia having been divorced as well but soon there was conflict. Unfortunately for me every time they would have their little breakups I would starve. Bad times.

I remember one large argument in particular was when Ben found out about Rick and that whenever my mother would break up with him, she would go out with Rick. So what Ben did was drive over to Rick's house and then he told him that he was sleeping with my mother. Oh yeah! I never told you about that particular incident right? Okay so Ben and my mother were together right? Ben had his own house but my mother said that it was too dirty and cluttered and how there was bad feng shui or some shit like that. She also didn't like going to motel rooms because they were even dirtier. So my mother decides to have sex with Ben in the room next to mine. Now this happened when I was going to college.

The last fucking thing that I want to come home to after working full time and going to school studying difficult medical classes is the sound of Ben and my mother having sex. I wasn't a peeper, I didn't want to bother them. I think that everyone is entitled to do whatever they want. Pursuit of happiness and all that shit. Why not? But I really can't tolerate it when I can't sleep because their bed is bouncing and making noises. That's a bit too extreme. Also the fact that my mother is moaning really doesn't help at all. Its those stupid American walls. Cheap drywall from China. Damn shoddy Chinese products.

But yes I could always hear them having sex. It sucked. Well maybe my mother did some but all I was concerned with at the time was the fact that I couldn't sleep. So I had to bang on pots and pans to get them to quiet down. It was really annoying, you know what I mean? The pots and pans were in the kitchen and I had to walk all the way downstairs to get them. Eventually I just got a stick and I hit the wall whenever they were too loud. So that was that. Now things got to an all time low. Both Ben and Rick broke up with my mother and I was starving. Fuck.

No problem at all! My mother got another boyfriend named Jim. He was in mortgages. He was a bit of a hipster to tell the truth but he also took us out to restaurants and brought food back to me so I liked him. There was something else that I never explained. Every summer when I had summer vacation I would go to visit my father. I had to go to the airport and I was excited because I would be nowhere near my mother. This one time when my mother was going out with Jim, she decided to ask (or force) Jim to send me to the airport. The airport was in New York so it was quite a long drive and my mother, Jim, and me would be going together.

We were getting ready to leave when all of a sudden Ben shows up out of nowhere. Apparently Ben had called my mother and tried to make up with her but she had decided at that point that she wouldn't bother with him anymore. Ben found out I was going to the airport because he had sent me to the airport before and met us right in front of the house. Ben made some gesture by buying me a book as a gift to read on the plane ride. Then he kissed my mother. In front of Jim.

During the car ride to the airport Jim was angry. I really didn't care because I knew my mother was like this and I had tried to warn her boyfriends but they didn't listen. Jim said that if he saw Ben again he would punch him in the face. I was dumbfounded at this because Ben and Jim were in their late forties and fifties. I could not believe that grown men were contemplating such a thing. Whatever. As long as I ate it was good enough for me and I didn't give a damn.

I think however Jim and my mother still were together. I don't know what excuse my mother came up with but it worked. Or she put out. Anyhow it greatly impacted me because they were buying groceries for me and I could actually eat. That's why I'm telling you all this. I think my mother didn't have sex with Jim because she said that he was short and bald. I was amazed at this because he was really nice to her and he was doing a lot for her. My mother doesn't appreciate shit.

When I say that he was short and bald, I mean that my mother was not sexually attracted to Jim. I thought that attraction comes from within. Apparently not. This affected me all my life because my mother kept telling me how I wasn't tall enough. I am currently five feet ten inches. I think I am just a little above the average US male height. I'm fucking Chinese this is great! I'm actually a decent height and I'm Chinese. My mother didn't think so.

She openly criticized me on my height and how that I should play basketball to grow taller. What a fucking idiot. This only contributed to my insecurity as a person but fortunately I tell her to fuck off whenever she dares to come up with such a stupid suggestion like that. I think basketball players are tall just because they are only ones who get picked, not because playing basketball makes people tall. That's akin to saying if a person cut off a finger, their children won't have the same finger that they cut off. Its completely crazy. Not to my mother. I was lucky to realize this, but how about if I didn't? After all I was only four years old when she started to tell me this. What a bitch.

So Jim finally washed out and my mother was single again. Ah well. By this time I was in the meltdown period in my freshman year. I didn't give a shit about anything. I decided that I would live with my father because the country he was retired in was relatively low cost and my mother had squandered all my college money. Oh yeah! I forgot to tell you how my mother lost all my college funds. Wait until you hear this.

CHAPTER 10

SOME RELIEF BUT NOT MUCH

DO you remember my father leaving me and my mother a good amount of money before he retired and escaped from my mother? Well my mother was supposed to use that money for my college tuition. My father told my mother and me that the money was specifically to be used for my education and that the rest should be invested so that we could also have some for expenses. I was ten years old but I still remember it clearly. So my mother stupidly lost all of the money in investments. That's why I'm so pissed. I know about the torture and all that, that's fine. However I could not deal with my future being robbed.

My mother also had a piece of real estate and apparently it got tied down and she was unable to sell it. Isn't that funny? She's a real estate broker and she can't sell a property. Her own property. No wonder we starved. Ironic.

So where was I going with this? Oh yeah I was talking about how I was going to live with my father in that low cost country of his. By the way this low cost country was China (surprise surprise!) and I decided to leave immediately since I had no future in the US if I wasn't able to find a job (this was during the start of the economic crisis in 2008). I tried to find work, trust me! I could not due to my inexperience or perceived inexperience and the fact that the economy was just starting to get bad then. In fact I had just quit my telemarketing job then because I couldn't make any sales since people were losing their entire life savings at the time.

I went to China. It was complete bliss. I enjoyed my time there. Nothing mattered to me. I was happy again. All because my mother wasn't there. I didn't even talk to her on the phone when I was there. I hung up if she called. I even got a job there and taught English to Chinese kids. Good times. I made many friends there and learned several languages including German, French, Russian, Korean, and Hungarian. I went to the beaches and basked in the sunset. I ate delicious Chinese food. I got a girlfriend. Really good times. I had a life. I had a job which was an immense boost to my self esteem and I was away from my mother. Then my visa expired. I had to return to the US.

Fuck. Shit. At this time I had spent roughly seventeen months in China and I forgot about my suicide attempts, my depression, and starvation. I really did! After all I was away from my mother. I was making a decent living there. I had fun there. I had a whole new life, I was starting anew. I had to return. They wouldn't extend my visa. I was desperate. I tried to renew my visa. Didn't work. I tried applying for citizenship. Didn't work, too complicated. I fucking had to go back and live with my mother. I was depressed again.

When I was in China I had communicated with my mother somewhat. I heard that she had a new boyfriend (what a surprise) called Harry and he was a banker or some shit like that. I didn't know much about this guy. Actually now that I remember more clearly, I met him. Yeah, it was right before I left for China. I met him about two weeks before I went to China to live with my father. He was nice. I remember also buying an airplane ticket and running to the bus station with all my luggage without telling my mother to escape. But that's irrelevant to my situation now. Now I had to come back and live with her.

What bullshit could she be bringing onto me? New wall molding to be installed? Go to a stupid real estate convention and be bored? No. Another boyfriend. Well I actually don't think they are called that now but whatever. His name was Joe. My mother had emailed me before I got back to the US and said that she and Joe would come and pick me up from the airport. Hmmm I thought. What the fuck is she going to pull on this guy? What suffering does Joe need to endure before this one is over? I don't know. Well we'll soon find out right?

So I was walking out of the airport gate (crying at the thought of my mother) and I saw them. They looked fairly happy together. "That'll last. Yeah, right!", I thought to myself when they walked up to me. Joe was nice and introduced himself. We then went home. This was a new one. We would be living with Joe and his family. "Wow", I thought to myself, my mother really put out this time. She must be massaging him AND sucking his dick I was thinking.

CHAPTER 11

A NEW START

SO we moved out of the apartment that my mother was renting at the time. The deal was that my mother, being a real estate broker, would set up her brokerage in one of Joe's businesses. Joe was impressed by my mother's credentials, and who wouldn't be. After my mother was a licensed real estate broker, and all that so why not? Joe was a businessman and had been in business for quite some time and he wanted to take a shot at this. It was intended that my mother would set up her brokerage and Joe would take a bit of the profit and at the same time they would be dating. Wow what a win-win situation right? WRONG!!!!!!!!!!!!!!!

I could see why Joe thought of this arrangement. Any business person would leap at this opportunity. Hell, I would! It was logical and had more benefits for everybody. It was great. Except for one thing. My mother.

We had to move from the apartment to Joe's house. Sounds simple right? No. I know moving is a stressful time for any human being. Things have to packed and labeled. Friends are being left behind. Familiar environments are being sacrificed. I know. There was more to it than that. The move, (drum roll) was planned by my mother. (Pause for mouth gaping) Now you know that this is going to be bad.

My mother, with her ingenious organization skills, her business savvy, her psychological prowess, was going to plan and organize a move. Yeah right. She couldn't organize a pile of leaves if she had to. She would probably just get someone else to do it for me, specifically me. So she calls the moving company and she gets the cheapest one. I can't blame her for that but she obviously didn't do the due diligence and ask what was required to do the move for so cheap. I'll tell you what we needed to do. We had to put all our things into boxes so that the moving company could move them according to their liability contract. Simple right?

My mother didn't get any boxes. Well she got maybe six or seven of them. We needed at least twenty or more to complete the moving. The moving company comes and they look around see that there are a lot of things that aren't in boxes. So they charged her for the boxes and tape. One box costs fifty dollars. One roll of tape costs ten dollars. It was a highway robbery. Actually it wasn't, and I will explain. The moving company already told my mother that everything had to be packed but she apparently didn't listen carefully enough. Her heads were in the clouds.

How does this affect me and Joe? We pay thirteen hundred dollars for the move and have to take a separate truck two times to the apartment just to finish the move. What a nightmare. So now my mother has these fucking wall frames that she wants to put up in the house. This is Joe's house. Out of his kindness we are living in his house on his property, and my mother is fucking around with wall frames. She wants us to put them up. This was the first time Joe had encountered my mother's unreasonable behavior. I simply ignored her. Joe was trying to be VERY polite and told my mother that he didn't want all that junk cluttering up HIS house. So my mother threw a temper tantrum.

She screamed, "NO RESPECT!", cried and didn't speak to Joe for a while. Joe started to have doubts about her business savvy and I tried to warn him about it. Of course he didn't believe my stories and he reacted in the manner that any normal people would react. "Its difficult being a single mother", "You should respect your mother for her efforts", "She is your mother and you should help her". I kept hearing these statements from Joe. I knew it was futile. Joe would soon find out the hard way. But back to the point.

CHAPTER 12

I CAN'T TAKE THIS SHIT ANYMORE

DO you remember the motherfucking toy thing that I hated? I was forced to build several of these things. I hated it. I cried. I screamed. I had to kneel in the dark for hours when I refused to do them. I was traumatized by them. My mother said it would let me train and that it was a life skill. I remember my mother telling me that I had to finish them by a certain time or else she would not let me go to sleep. I went without food or water until I finished the segment she wanted me to. She would spank me if I still refused. What a bitch.

Now these motherfucking toy things are in Joe's house. Joe has the acumen to note that these old fucking pieces of garbage should belong where they belong. In the garbage. I pleaded with her to get rid of them but she of course refused. The motherfucking toy things were really a fucking eyesore. Joe had redone the living room and put in hardwood floors. (This was a separate house by the way and he had five buildings on his property) He had spent about six thousand dollars on the hardwood floor just to make it nice for my mother and me to live in.

I naturally didn't require it. Shit, I could live in a cave, so long as it had heat, a door, and food. My mother wanted it all. I was in despair as I realized that I had such a great opportunity to live rent free in Joe's house because my mother was testing his limits. I really think my mother gets a thrill out of this stupid bullshit she creates. It feeds her mentally. She thrives on drama. She also thrives on bossing other people around. The only reason Joe put up with my mother was because of the business interest which was why he put up with this nonsense.

So these motherfucking toy things are in the house and they are taking up space in the living room. They are old, unsightly, and collapsing on themselves. Joe and I discuss the stupidity of this and my mother's insistence that they be kept around. We then attempt to come up with a way to get rid of these things. I first proposed that we make it look as if they were stolen by someone. However we realize that we would have to pay someone to even take them, being that they are so useless. Then we try reasoning with my mother which was a waste of time. She kept saying, "NO RESPECT!" and about how they were hers and that we needed to respect her property. These damn things are a reminder of my traumatic childhood.

Joe paid for my airline ticket back from Asia. He let us live rent free in his house. He even bought groceries for us. He is a great guy. He also had his family on the property. His parents and daughter also lived on with him. I feel sorry for this family. I really do. They had to encounter my mother and interact with her.

On with my story. The real estate deal with Joe was that my

mother would provide a center for apartment rentals and they would get commission from that. Really simple. All my mother had to do was transfer her license over to the new address, hire some real estate agents, and send them out to do the work. This never came to fruition due to my mother's procrastination. I don't know what it was but it was probably because my mother sucks.

Joe paid for my airline ticket back because my mother told him that I would be one of those agents who would work in the real estate business. I would go to real estate school and get licensed so that I could produce income as soon as possible. It didn't happen. By this time it was late 2010 and the real estate industry was nowhere. There weren't even any real estate schools holding courses because of the lack of students. Also my mother was not doing any work to prepare for the business. This scared Joe who was to invest in the business.

After several weeks of not working and waiting for nothing to happen, I decided to join the military. I felt that it was the only way for me to build my future and for me to escape from my mother. I wanted to join the army. So I went to the recruiter and they told me all about the pay, the benefits, and the honor that was soon to be bestowed upon me when I joined. I went through all the processing and the paperwork. I went to the station to do the exam and got a very high score on it. Everything looked rosy and I was feeling optimistic again. Then I failed the medical exam.

I actually didn't fail it but my records disqualified me from joining. Technically I could get in but it was risky and I decided not to do it. Remember at the beginning of the book when I mentioned about my suicide attempts, hospitalization, and examinations by the psychologists? Yeah, that disqualified me. The military absolutely shuns those with a history of mental health issues particularly those with suicidal thoughts. I just wanted to make a living. I didn't really want to kill myself if I could. I only had suicidal thoughts at the time because the pressure from my mother was simply too great. After I began ignoring her I felt much better. But now my chance to escape was compromised. I had to return home.

A couple of months passed by. I was gearing to go back to China because this shit was not working out. I was supposed to have a job in the real estate business. I was supposed to join the army. So I wanted to go back to China and get the hell away from my mother. There was another hurdle for me. I couldn't get the proper documentation to go back. So now I was really stuck there. I had to see my mother everyday. Painful. I felt like killing myself again. Even though I completely ignored her and flipped her off as much as I could, I was desolate because I had just started to see a light at the end of the tunnel but it faded away. Hard times.

Joe was not much enthusiastic about the status quo. Now he was feeding and housing two people who were supposed to produce income for him. He wasn't an asshole but economics are economics. "If you don't make money, how are you going to pay for the expenses?" he asked my mother. I agreed, after all it is expensive to live in the United States. That's reality. He told me to find a job. That proved much harder than it sounded. It would take me more than 550 tries to get a job. I finally got a job, at the aforementioned donut shop. But it took nearly two and a half months to do so. During that time, I literally did nothing and sat in my room staring at the wall, waiting for a potential employer to call me for a job interview. That sucked.

Actually I had a job offer earlier on. The call was from some gas station and they were looking to hire people to be gas pump attendants. I remember how thrilled I was at the prospect of having even the chance to go to the interview. I told Joe about the job enthusiastically and he supported it. After all it was something so that I could at least pay for groceries and gas. The recruiter had just called and I was dressed and ready to go out the door when my mother stopped me. She had overheard the conversation and forbade me to do that job. Joe and I were surprised.

"You mean you're not going to let him pump gas while you fucking don't even have an income?", Joe said. He was dumbfounded. I was too. The economy was bad enough that people were lucky to even keep their jobs and here I was being offered a job. We tried to talk to my mother again to explain the desperate situation I was in. Joe was saying, "let the kid get some money in his pocket, he doesn't have to do it for the rest of his life", but my mother would have none of it. She said that I could not work at a gas station because the stigma would psychologically damage me. I was like, "What fucking stigma?! I need to fucking eat, you do too! Who the fuck do you think is paying for our groceries now?" but my mother was deadset in not allowing me to get that job. So then I said to her, "suck my cock", and I walked out the door to go for the interview.

She threatened to not allow me to use her car from then on if I went to the interview. Joe and I were going fucking crazy at this, as we could not believe what we were hearing. I told my mother to fuck off and I went, while Joe talked to her and tried to reason with her, thinking that she may have misapprehended the situation. She didn't. My mother genuinely believed that I should not take the job because it was not a status symbol of success. I should be a doctor or a real estate mogul and pumping gas was a job for poor people she had said and I went berserk at that. Joe stood up for me and they got into a fight over that. Just over that issue. The fight wasn't even about them, it was about me being prevented from getting some money from a job. My mother went into one of her tantrums when Joe asked her where the money was coming from to pay her bills. He would only tolerate so much. So they didn't speak to each other for a week after that fight. She is not only fucking crazy but her brain must have been burned or something like that. Fortunately I got a job later at a donut shop because otherwise I would have been in bad shape.

My mother also had the nerve to suggest that I be an entre-preneur and start my own business. It sounded logical but keep reading, it wasn't. She suggested that I open my own daycare service for young children and baby sit them for money. I thought that was not such a bad idea but the only problem was that I had not much experience doing that. Then she said that the daycare service should center around me teaching the chil-dren to build motherfucking toy things that I hated structures. Joe and I thought that she had really gone over the edge at that point. "What the hell? You need that business advice like you need a bullet in your head," Joe told my mother. I agreed, it sounded so bad that I didn't even stay listen to what she had to say in her rebuttal. Apparently everything makes sense to her and every one else is just plain stupid. My mother, in her warped sense of thinking is always right. No matter what. I wish I could be there when a cop pulls her over for speeding. It would be interesting to say the least. So they got into another fight and didn't speak to each other for a week again. (Don't worry, this time my mother isn't going anywhere. After all she's living in Joe's house and eating food that his money buys.)

Remember the piano, violin, trumpet, and drum lessons I took as a child? Well finally these instruments seemed to be able to become usable. The lessons sucked but now Joe suggested that we could sell all of them which were just lying around the house, taking up space. I remember the conversation that we had with my mother. "Let that poor kid sell the instruments and get a couple of bucks," Joe said. My mother's rebuttal, "No respect! Those are MY instruments". Joe then asks, "Do you play them at all?" and my mother answers, "No". You can see how fucking crazy she is. She never even learned how to properly play the instruments. My mother can't even read a fucking note to play the violin yet she wants to keep the stupid instruments while I don't have a job and our expenses are piling up. What a fucking psychopath!

Chapter 13

My new extended family

I should tell you about how Joe's family felt about all of this craziness. Joe's family is comprised of his parents and his daughter. We would have dinner with them on a regular basis. This is where things got interesting. Up to this point I never got a good perspective about how other people viewed my mother. This is because they have not been with her long enough to know every detail about her. When I mean long enough, I mean actually living with her. I lived with her for over twenty years so far, I can tell you it's a nightmare. However, I am desensitized to her ramblings. I know what to expect from her. I know her stubbornness. I know that she is completely useless at taking orders. I know that she attempts to defy logic and reason at every chance that she gets. She is a drama queen. She is demanding and overbearing. I know all that. But other people don't.

Most people who have met my mother only meet her briefly. Perhaps for business, or dating. This type of encounter does not give a person an accurate assessment of my mother's personality. I fact they only mystify them. Many people actually think highly of my mother because they only see the surface of her behavior. Some even think that she is a very intelligent and powerful person who is very successful as a result. Bullshit. She simply inflates herself to that but never achieves it. She is like a paper tiger. Her image is not consummate with her actions or attitude. It is highly misleading. That is why Joe gave her the opportunity to get ahead. That is why Joe let her and me live rent free for several months. She kept delaying him with seemingly logical reasons and still does. What a bitch.

Back to where I was going with this. Other people don't know my mother at all. However now, Joe's family was about to be the first to encounter her diva personality. I hope they don't kill themselves.

Joe himself was a very nice guy. I like him. He reminds me of my father, hard working, adaptable, but I feel sorry for him because he had to meet my mother. Joe was also a very talented person. He was a businessperson but he also had hobbies on the side. He enjoyed collecting antique cars, fixing the aforementioned cars, and many other activities. One particular hobby of his was an invention. He had invented and patented a vapor less toilet bowl. Apparently this device was odorless, but I didn't believe it until I tried it. It worked like magic. The damn thing had a neat little motor fan built into it that sucked out the odors into a pipe that led into a sewer. What an invention! The whole time I was taking a dump I did not smell anything in the bathroom. Quiet too. I'll never forget it. I remember Joe saying that he had tried to look for a similar invention but could not find one so he patented it and had one made. Amazing stuff.

Unfortunately I can't use it everyday since its in his house. I tried sneaking into his house one day just to use it and set off the house alarm. Awkward. That's how much I dug that invention of his.

Let's talk about Joe's daughter. We'll call her Allison. Sure. Allison was one of those girls who didn't take shit. She was very nice, in fact I rather liked her strong willed personality. She had an admirable confidence about her that I lacked all my life and coveted. Allison's difference from my mother was that she actually had a brain and knew how other people felt. Unlike my mother of course who was a sociopath and didn't care about the reactions of other people. There was a clash between them as you will see.

First let me explain the situation around Joe's family. Joe was a very smart, nice, and business savvy guy. He treated people respectfully but also saw attention to detail. He was one of the most ideal people I have seen in regards to humanity. Unfortunately, people tried to take advantage of his sympathetic views. His wife in particular committed adultery on him and hurt him terribly. To add insult to injury, this relationship had gone on for about two years. The man Joe's wife was cheating with was also his best friend. What a sad story.

This allowed Joe to see past my mother's bitchiness and that's why he didn't and hasn't fallen for my mother's diva like behavior. He was now separated from his wife and wanted to start anew. So he found my mother through an online dating website and being that his wife (the one who had committed adultery) was Asian, he found my mother particularly appealing.

Joe's family was deeply hurt and shocked by his wife. They were a very family oriented type of people and were heavily impacted by this. So my mother comes into the picture and she sucks.

Joe's parents also lived on the property with him. His mother, lets call her Betty, was a very kind and considerate woman. She was in her late seventies and had to work at Joe's business, and take care of her husband, Joe's father, uh, Carl, due to his Alzheimer's. Betty was a very traditional woman. She worked, cooked, cleaned, did everything. I admire her for that. She earned my respect for her behavior.

So now my mother waltzes in on the scene. I cringe at her every behavior because it impacts me deeply. Even though I don't care about her or listen to her anymore, my food, bed, and well being are stake because of Joe. After all, I am living rent free in his house. And my mother has the nerve to be a "Tiger mother" towards them. I am truly scared because should Joe decide to kick us out, I'll be hungry again, only this time without shelter.

Joe is not the type of person who would do that. But due to the way my mother behaves, I believe that no human being would tolerate it. You see, my mother is a "Tiger mother" to everyone. She thinks that the world owes her a living. Or maybe its because she sucks. The way she treats me is reflected on the way she treats others. Drama is rising.

Remember I mentioned earlier that Betty, Joe's mother, cooked and cleaned. Well she was a traditional type of woman from an Italian family. This family ate, worked, and did everything together. Very close knit and tight. I admire them, it is a good trait to have. So now my mother comes in and she acts the same way in front of this family as she does in front of me.

I will give you an example. One night we are having dinner, courtesy of Betty and my mother has the nerve to tell Betty that the beef was undercooked. Chinese people don't really have the concept of eating things raw. I suppose traditionally that was because they wanted to kill all the airborne bacteria in food so they were never raw. My mother is disgusted at this and she orders Betty to cook the food again just for her. Hmmm, well needless to say, Betty was taken back. No, Betty was shocked at this. But she said nothing and did what my mother told her to do. She wanted to be polite to my mother.

So after everyone cringed, especially me, at this abhorrent behavior, my mother decides that she is full and that she would like to go back to her house (there are three houses on Joe's property). She does not even consider helping Betty with the dishes because that responsibility is mine and Betty's. Later, she tells Betty that I will do the dishes from now on because, "Derrick needs to learn". Now like I said, Betty is a woman in her late seventies. She works ten hours a day, buys food, cooks food, and then repeats this six days a week. She also has to take care of Carl, who has Alzheimer's. My mother is such a goddamn bitch.

This incident was not isolated. In fact when we have dinner everyday, my mother also did the same thing. She shied away from doing any work whatsoever and ordered other people to do it for her. Did I tell you how she got to be a part of this family? Joe is being very generous. He let me and my mother live there and let us experience what a family is like. He purposely let us live there rent free so that we could build a better future for ourselves after my mother SQUANDERED the money my father gave her. I think she spent most of it on breast implants and facelifts because her breasts look too big for a four foot eleven Asian woman in proportion.

I think my mother has some psychological problem about her. I am not saying that all Chinese mothers are bad. I am not saying that being a "Tiger mother" is completely unaccept-able. I simply think that I personally don't like it. My mother is a "Tiger mom" and I think that she is a piece of shit. Just look at how she treated me. But also look at how she treated other people. Being a good mother, one should encourage and push their children. That why they will become responsible and better, I think. But this! My mother just sucks. I feel sorry for any other people in my situation. Because they don't like this form of parenting just as I don't. My opinion is that it IS abuse. It IS traumatic. The only reason why I haven't killed myself is because now I have found a defense mechanism to avoid further pain. I simply ignore my mother and insult her as much as I can to avoid committing suicide. I need to do it now. If I don't I really would kill myself. That's how painful it is. I can take it. I have lived this my whole life. But, I don't think other people can. On with my story.

I mentioned that Joe's daughter Allison, did not take shit. What I mean is that she was very strong willed. In Joe's own words, "she's a ball buster". Too bad she can't literally kick me in the balls because that's what gets me off. Nah, I'm just kidding. Allison has a boyfriend. I respect people for who they are. But let me describe how inconsiderate and overbearing my "Tiger mother" is to other people.

Joe had been through tough times. His wife had cheated on him and they were now separated. This affected everyone especially Allison. She had grown up her whole life in a very family like setting and this was a slap in the face for her. I have sympathy for Allison. I really do. Of course I don't feel the same way with my parents because I was glad my father divorced my mother. The situation with my father was much more different being that he had been nothing more to her but an ox to be worked until death. I was more than supportive of my father's decision because I was aware of the suffering that was associated with my mother.

My mother has this mentality that she should fill the position of Allison's biological mother now that she is separated the family. She starts her "Tiger motherness" on Allison. My mother tells Allison to clean the house, to wash the dishes, to do the laundry, and to study for hours on end. It was fun to watch, I laughed a lot. Allison initially tried be polite. She told my mother that she did not appreciate her trying to take her biological mother's place. She then told her father, Joe, about this. Allison was eighteen at the time but my mother still treated her like a child. No, in fact my mother treats everyone as if they were children. She is the supreme figure over everyone human being. Everyone has to answer to her and show respect to her regardless of whatever she does. So my mother approached Allison to tell her that she was a "spoiled brat". She said that

Allison should go and do drugs and party because that's all that she could aspire to be. Therefore Allison punched her in the face.

I could not stop laughing. I thought it was so funny. I could not punch my own mother, just because she is my own mother because I would feel guilty even though I hate her guts. But Allison could. In fact Allison was a fourth degree black belt in Taekwondo. She kicked my mother's ass. It was epic. My mother was laying on the ground and crying for help. Joe was shocked and went to help my mother because he was dating her. I rolling around laughing. I thought it was hilarious. I wished I had filmed it because then I would put it up on the internet and title as, "Bitch mother got what she had coming to her", and told anyone who I knew to watch it. I would have probably gotten over a million hits if I did. Good times.

So now my mother is crying and so forth and I am laughing. Joe is giving Allison a stern talking to but I am supporting Allison. In fact I am fan of hers to tell you the truth for doing that. Allison did what I could not do my entire life. She gave it to my mother. Its moment like these that give me the will to live. To see my mother slapped, literally and metaphorically in the face. Because she sucks.

CHAPTER 14

MY INTERESTS AND PAST TIME HOBBIES

WHY don't I tell you some of the hobbies that I developed as a result of this type of upbringing. What kind of hobbies do you think that a person like me might be interested in? After all I was raised to study for hours on end, forced to do all household chores for myself and my mother, write checks, and be forced to get grades no lower than an A. At least that was the expectation of me.

My hobbies include learning foreign languages, reading technical books, looking at old training movies, photography, watching pornography of women beating men, and having sex. When I was living in China, I met a lot of foreigners and took the time there learn as many foreign languages as I could. I think I mentioned the ones I learned before but my point is that I was very open to meeting people and learning about different cultures. I guess reading books and watching old instructional films aren't of much interest but I like them.

I actually got interested in learning foreign languages

because I was a bit homesick (not for my mother) about the United States when I was living in China for such a long period of time. Any foreign looking person that I came across, I usually talked to. They were surprised that a Chinese person would speak such fluent English until I told them that I was born in the United States. I made a lot of friends there but as soon I came back to the United States I was too depressed to keep up with them as I explained earlier.

Do you have a relative in your family who is famous? I do. It's quite humorous when I look at my ancestors. My father's grandfather was a Chinese general. Essentially he was in command of about 5,000 soldiers. This was during the last Chinese dynasty and when the government collapsed, he joined the Nationalists. My biological grandfather was a doctor who was trained by American people. He helped fight the Japanese during the second world war. When those Americans who trained him left China after the war ended, they gave him the hospital that he was stationed at. As a result he had all the modern medical supplies left behind, especially penicillin. At the time there were many warlords who had STDs and they would usually come to my grandfather to get cured. After giving them penicillin and them feeling better, the warlords usually gave my grandfather a chest or two of gold coins. Now I'm talking about a chest that must have weighed at least a couple hundred pounds. That's how wealthy they were.

Then the civil war came and my grandfather died. My father then grew up poor as hell and eventually immigrated to the US from Taiwan. Pretty simple stuff. My father had to learn to live on his own as there was almost no infrastructure or education in Taiwan after the devastation of World War two. My father joined the military at a young age to escape the poverty and hunger of the streets. He then joined the special forces and stayed there for several years. It was a hard life for him but he pulled through and eventually immigrated to the United States. That might explain the reason how he managed to deal with my mother so long, he had been through hardship before and it did not faze him as it did me or other people.

How about my mother's side you say? Patience, dear reader! Patience! Okay so my mother sucks but that's not what I am trying to talk about here. I'm talking about fame in the bloodline. Hmmm…… the only famous person that I can think of on my mother's side is one of her nieces. She is a singer in Taiwan and she is about as popular in Asia as any superstar. Well she was. Her career started in 1998 so she's kind of had her run by now. I don't really have much negative things to say about her. When I met her she was busy. Not mean, just busy and I can't judge someone for that.

In fact, let me tell you the reason why I don't feel any negativity towards them in particular. My mother's parents kind of suck too. I guess its in their genes to suck. Anyhow, I was told by my singer cousin that her family was evicted by the parents. My grandparents, or my mother's parents, lets call them Ching and Chong. So Ching and Chong own a company called Motherfucker Company. They decide to let one of their sons, my famous cousin's father (lets call him Jerry), operate and manage one of their buildings. So he opens the store and it is successful. I think they sold eyeglass frames or some shit like that. Anyhow, Ching and Chong apparently have their, "face" (or in American terms, pride) bashed when Jerry's wife, (lets call her Britney) Britney decides that she has no time to have dinner with them and instead makes bento boxes for them. So Ching and Chong are apparently insulted, thinking that they were treated like dogs, and decide to evict Jerry and Britney from the building. Jerry and Britney have put hard work into their thriving business and now they are getting their asses kicked out. This all culminates in a lawsuit. Ching and Chong won. Wow, my mother's family really sucks. Except for the ones I said who didn't suck of course. I once asked Ching about this and she said that Jerry was being too greedy and had, "no respect" for them. So I said, "suck my cock", took the money she was giving me and left. I don't think I will be going back soon. Fortunately my grandmother doesn't speak English but I think that when I flipped her off she kind of got the gist of that.

Fortunately for Jerry and Britney they got vindication for the suffering that Ching and Chong put them through. Jerry's daughter (lets call her Kelly) was fond of singing as a child. In fact she even sang songs in English which was a feat considering that this was in Taiwan where the official language is not English. Kelly went to a singing contest and won when she was about eighteen years old. A talent agent noticed her and she became a famous singer there. Talk about a slap in the face for Ching and Chong. So after this fame and fortune, guess who's not getting a fruit cake at Christmas time? Ching and Chong of course. In fact, Jerry and Britney don't even talk to them anymore as of now.

My mother, being the freeloader that she is, suddenly started to suck up to her brother Jerry and his wife Britney.

Before when my father was doing well, my mother had her head stuck up to the sky but now, she had to kiss their asses because they were richer than her. Before Kelly got famous, her older sister (lets call her Sarah) had stayed over at our home. My father treated her quite well being the generally kind person he is and Sarah had fond memories of how she was treated. My mother on the other hand was jealous because she believed that my father was having an affair but could not prove it at the time. This was years before the divorce but my father already hated the bull shit my mother was pulling.

Why didn't he just take off then you ask? At the time his business was doing very well and I suppose he had no need to do so. It is interesting for me to see how my mother was jealous of Sarah despite the fact that my father at the time was working like an ox and did not even have time to be with me. My point being that unlike Ching and Chong, Jerry and Britney thought of our family as having a neutral stance. We were in the United States so we had nothing to do with the ugly incident with the Motherfucker company and the litigation that Ching Chong and Jerry were involved in. That was the only reason why I got to see my famous cousin and live in her house for a few weeks. Then my mother decided that she wanted to kiss their asses and get benefits from them. That's when Jerry and Britney rightfully stopped answering the phone calls.

It did not really faze me but I was pissed off that my mother would be so inconsiderate of other people. I personally did not care about their fame. It did not affect me. Good for them. I did not want anything from them and thought of them as decently as I could. Why should I mooch off of them? Evidently my mother didn't think so. She kept pressuring me to go to their house, go out with them, and try to establish good relations with them so that she would be able to derive benefits from them. I told her how I felt about her intentions to suck up by saying, "suck my cock", and then ignoring her.

CHAPTER 15

GOOD TIMES IN CHINA

I think you must be curious about my life in China. After all I did not say much about what happened during my time there other than the fact that I enjoyed it because my mother was not there. Why don't I fill you in on that period of my blissful life. There were some bumps during that journey but it wasn't so bad. In fact, I will go so far as to say that those bumps and tribulations that I encountered were healthy and made me a better person.

So I had met a lot of foreigners in China and I got to be friends with a lot of them. I remember in particular the Canadians, who kept explaining to me how they hated Americans due to their ignorance and war making tendencies and then watching them shut up when I told them that I was an American. There were the Germans who loved dancing all night in "discos" as they called it, the usually drunk Russians who were distant from others otherwise, Chinese people of course, a couple of cool Frenchmen and French women, and even some Hungarians come to think of it.

We were all expatriates and came together through the

mutual status of being foreigners there. I made some very good friends. One in particular was a British guy with a crazy Mohawk. Let's call him Mike. I forget what city Mike was from but all I knew what that when Mike got to China, he was only sober for one day during the first two months he arrived to China. He taught me how to go nightclubbing and how to dance. He also introduced me to alcohol. The legal age to drink in China is eighteen so I got drunk for the first time in my life. It was great.

Mike however calmed down somewhat after he met a girl from a Scandinavian country called (lets call her Monica) Monica. Monica, hmm, I don't remember much about her. She was cool. Yup good enough. However I got to be very good friends with a Frenchman. Lets call him John Smith. John Smith was a magician and we hung out a lot. Along with John, there was another Frenchman (I'll call him Harry) who made a living by playing online poker. Oh and there were Russians too. One particular chap who I could not help but take liking to was from Moscow. (I shall call him Dimitri) Dimitri always had a smile on his face and was usually laughing. His Chinese was quite fluent for a foreigner and I liked his sense of humor. He told me the merits of drinking Vodka instead of Whisky so as to avoid a bad hangover. I also met a Russian couple there who had been married and were living in China. Though I met them during the period of time when I was about to return for the US, I was very touched by their hospitality. The husband made his living as a translator and his wife was a homemaker. It was a medley of interesting people there, one after another.

With all these foreigners I was never bored there. However

that was also the first time I fell in love, or so I thought. There was a Korean girl there (lets call her Kim) and I was learning Korean at the time so I thought it would be befitting for us to try to arrange a language exchange. Dimitri had introduced me to her and thought that it would be cute to see us together. We got to know each other well and I felt love for the first time in my life. So I have never felt this feeling before and I take Kim out on a couple of dates. We go to the park, to the beach, and other couple type of stuff. She made me feel like I had never felt before. I never felt so happy before in my life. It was as if the wounds from those years of suffering under my mother had been healed. It was a shame because this dream did not last very long. You know, with my mother emasculating me and all that shit, I have a warped sense of thinking due to the psychological damage that I had.

It started off one day when I picked Kim up from her dormitory. I couldn't think of anything to do so I suggested that we go back to my house. I decide to put on a movie after we get there and Kim is completely horrified. I am no sociologist but I know that a lot of Asian people usually are much more conservative than European or North American people. Its part of the culture and I had forgot at that point. Actually that's not an excuse for what I did. I was just so deranged from the trauma that my mother caused that at the time I didn't even think about my actions. It wasn't an ordinary movie that I put on, it was one of my pornographic films. Also it was the one where the women were whipping the men. So Kim now is terrified at this and she just leaves my house. She doesn't even want me to send her home. I didn't even put the video in as a joke, I actually thought it would entertain her in some way. I guess I was wrong.

I tried calling her but she refused to see me ever again. Thanks a lot mother. However as I think about that now, it's quite funny. I was fell into a gloom after that, realizing what I had just done, because Kim was so beautiful and I actually felt something good for the first time in my life. For the next three weeks I was sober for about a day after that. I printed the pictures that I had taken of her and with her. I enlarged them and put them on my walls. I made smaller ones and wore them in a necklace at all times. I went for long walks to nowhere, often times with a bottle of whiskey. I went insane about Kim and how I had lost her.

Finally John Smith and Mike Jones helped me out. My friends had gotten wind of what had happened and came to save me from myself. It was after the period of three weeks where I didn't shower, shave, or eat as a result of the drinking that I finally decided to go outside and find Kim. I ended up going to a club where there were a bunch of Chinese students practicing their English. Dimitri happened to be there because he was trying to practice his Chinese and he saw the state I was in. I had been drinking during my way there and I could not walk in a straight line. Then I thought I saw a girl who looked like Kim and I lunged towards her. Dimitri managed to wrestle me to the ground and knock the bottle out of my hand. He then called John and Mike and they came to take me to Dimitri's apartment where I couldn't hurt myself. According to them, I passed out on the floor there. When I woke up, they told me to snap out of it. They told me stories about their past mishaps with women and how I should forget about Kim. I got through it with some "magic" from John. No literally, John Smith performed magic for me. He made cards disappear, he blew coins out of his nose, and he made empty boxes of cigarettes full. After that they started to take me to parties, to the beach, to anywhere where I could take my mind off of Kim. After another week, I managed to pull myself back together. What nice friends.

This was healthy. Unlike my perpetual depression with the thought of my mother, that incident with the Korean girl was a normal depression if I might say. Ah well, that life is gone and done. I got a lot of experience about the finer things that I missed the time I was there. So that is basically what happened in China, I taught English to Chinese kids, I made friends, I danced at nightclubs, I fell in love, I got rejected, I got drunk, I sobered up, I danced some more, and my visa expired so I had to return to the US. Good times.

Chapter 16

Good times in the US

ACTUALLY, I had friends in the United States. Come on, I still had a few friends even though my mother did not allow me to have sleepovers or play dates. We met at school. I will always remember the good times we had when I was still oblivious to the abuse my mother was doing to me. I remember my earliest friend. I have known him since we were four years old. I will call him Charles here. I remember him in particular because of one great act of kindness he did for me.

My mother would always buy me a school lunch because she was lazy. The school lunches when I was in middle school were inedible. They were horrible. I could not believe that the food was allowed to be distributed. I had no choice but to eat them. I was hungry all the time because I refused to eat them. Charles helped me. He gave me half of his pastrami sandwich almost everyday for several years. Sometimes he would even bring me a juice box and even cookies. What a friend. I don't know what happened to him but I am grateful for his kindness and I will strive to show him my appreciation somehow.

There was also another friend that I met when I was in high

school. Let's call him Jake. This was later on just before I went to college. We had met in high school and got to be fairly good pals, having the same interests. He was always making jokes about Asians in general and I eventually got to like his sense of humor. I would usually pretend to be a cook at a Chinese restaurant and whenever he would call me I would go, "ah ching chong chong! You want flied rice?", and he would simply roll on the floor laughing at that.

The most memorable time I had with Jake was with his other friend (Keith) and when he invited me one day after school to go somewhere with him and Keith. I was reluctant to go, having the mentality that my mother never let me go play with my friends, but my mother was much more lax with me at this point seeing that I had already been accepted into a state college. So I went with them to Jake's house. Or so that where I thought we were supposed to go.

Keith had this yellow hatchback with a sunroof and bicycle racks on the roof. He was a pretty good driver and could do several stunts with the car. After shitting myself when he tried to drift the car in a parking lot, Jake asked me to get out of the car with him. We were at an elementary school parking lot and Jake said that he had to go pick up his sister. Only that he did not have a sister. I asked him about this and when I turned around, Jake was bolting back to the car. I ran after Jake and tried to stop him but now Jake was motioning to Keith to floor the car and drive off without me.

I was freaked out about this so I quickly caught hold of the bicycle rack and hung on. Keith tried to throw me off balance by speeding and then making several turns. I managed to get onto the roof of the car and I got in through the sunroof. This would be our signature move. I hated driving so Keith would usually drive when Jake and I hung out and they would try and pull that same move on me every time. One time it got a bit too far when we had just finished eating and Keith tried to take off without me.

We were supposed to pull the stunt on Jake and I was in on it but Keith decided to switch dupes and I was to be the one stranded instead. This time however, I hung onto the bike rack but Keith just kept driving. We eventually were driving on the highway and doing sixty miles per hour before they stopped and let me in the car. I suppose this is what you might call, a small period of fun during my youth.

Chapter 17

More hobbies

ITS not always painful to be around my mother. I try to have as much fun as I possibly can given the situation and there are other instances where I manage to get a few laughs out of my ordeal. I usually tell this story to people who will listen. I was two years old when I first viewed an adult film. I mean pornography.

At the time I thought there was a Caucasian woman eating some grapes and I thought nothing more of it. It was all that my thought process could fathom, after all I was only two years old. However now I realize that there was an African American man being given a blowjob by the aforementioned Caucasian female. I mention this because as traumatized or repressed as I am about my life due to my bitch mother, at least I am sexually mature.

Ironically my mother was the one who taught me to be comfortable with my own body and that I should not be ashamed of being naked. Therefore I tend not to be ashamed when it comes to discussions about sex. So let me give you an instance where I make light of an awkward situation. I first discovered pornographic films and their benefits when I was ten years old. The regular sex did not interest me at all. Then I saw pictures of women who were beating men.

I was fascinated by this concept of women terrorizing and emasculating men sexually. Now that I think about it I think that I may very well like this concept of sadomachoism because of my mother always controlling me. I'm no expert but this is my opinion. My main point is that I enjoy this pornographic material that relates somehow to women dominating men sexually. It is called femdom. I also like SM, whipping, chains, high heels, and generally scenes of women sexually dominating men. My mother thought I was insane when she saw me looking at this material.

I remember I was looking at a high heel fetish website one day and my mother suddenly confronted me. She was shocked and found out that I was going on the websites because I had recently got her computer infected with many and she found out from the computer technician about the internet activity there. She was horrified that I was enjoying the scenes of women beating men and told me that I was crazy. So she made an appointment with a psychologist.

Though my mother told me not to look at those websites or material anymore, I still did. In fact I still do right now. Anyhow I would also masturbate to that type of genre of pornographic materials. What can I say it gets me off. My mother accidentally chanced upon me when I was masturbating. When I was younger I would masturbate on the floor and press my groin against it. So imagine me lying on the floor and my mother walks in. She is horrified by the sight of me doing it and screams at me to stop. Naturally I did but as soon as she walked out I finished what I was doing.

Before I went to the psychologist my mother told me that I would have a heart attack if I kept masturbating. She also said that it would stunt my growth and all these other bad things. Goddamn bitch. Why the fuck should she interfere with orgasms. They feel good. Anyhow I still masturbated because I didn't give a damn. Finally came the appointment with the psychologist.

I remember that it was quite uneventful and the first meeting consisted of nothing but the psychologist writing down my information on a chart. The second meeting was much juicier. I actually knew at the time that my fetish with femdom, feet, high heels, and SM was normal. I had read in an encyclopedia that it was nothing out of the ordinary. So the psychologist first asked me a bunch of questions about my life. He asked about if what food I liked, where I grew up etc. Then he held up a series of pictures. They were ink blots and he asked me to tell him what came to my mind when I saw them.

After this assessment, he asked me what I usually thought about. I said, "sex". He was a bit surprised and asked me what else I thought about. He assumed that I misunderstood the question and so he asked me about how I felt about myself. I talked about my fascination with women beating men and how I especially liked it when they wore high heels and trampled men in them.

After the session the psychologist told me that I was a normally functioning young boy and that there was nothing to worry about. So that was the end of that. But my mother was still frightened and she tried to stop me from masturbating to that material by refusing to allow on the computer.

I was quite annoyed by that but there was nothing I could do about it. So I resorted to masturbating at department store catalogs and women's magazines. Yeah why not? I just employed my imagination that the women were naked and that they are beating me or saying demeaning things to me. It was simple! The funny moments eventually came when my mother would go into my room while I was masturbating without her knowledge. When she came in the room I immediately shouted, "Get the fuck out! I'm masturbating", and she would be very shocked and go away. Only afterwards would she try to punish me and later on not at all. I think that overwhelmed her because she wasn't a man. Unfortunately she stopped subscribing to those magazines. What a killjoy!

Later on when I was in high school, I was able to access my mother's computer. She was dating and would usually be gone for hours at a time so I gleefully ran to her room to download as many pornographic SM films as I could. I remember one incident when she brought one of her boyfriends home and I was masturbating on her computer. I don't mean that I was ejaculating onto her computer, I mean that I was masturbating to movies on her computer because she had a flat screen monitor that was bigger than mine at the time. I was so angry that they had come home early so I shouted, "Fuck off, I'm not finished masturbating and I just found some really good ones here!".

After that my mother put a password on her computer. Fuck. I had to resort back to the magazines for a while there.

During that incident I couldn't imagine the reaction on her boyfriend's face but I was really pissed off because it had taken me a long time to find this specific movie where the adult actress was kicking a man in the balls with high heel boots on. Those movies aren't easy to find so you can imagine the frustration I experienced when I couldn't enjoy it. And it wasn't always that my mother would be out of the house so that only made things worse. Sometimes my mother would go out to a business meeting that would only last for twenty minutes. As soon as I heard her car pull up, I had to quickly disengage. One time I didn't hear her car pull up because she had to find parking farther away. It was not until she had opened the door that I realized she was home earlier than I expected. I cummed all over the keyboard and floor as a result of being caught off guard that one time. I got wise to it though and later on I asked how long she would be gone for before doing that and having to clean up with a rubbing alcohol dampened paper towel. It was the clear type of rubbing alcohol, not the green one. I learned that hydrogen peroxide only damages the surface of things so I didn't use that. Fun times. Now I have my own computer so I don't have to worry about it. It's got a very high definition monitor. My dick is much more sore more often now than when I was young. It's like evolution to me, adapt to the situation and evolve.

MY THOUGHTS

FROM information that I have gathered from relatives and other people, I can summarize why I think the hard line approach can damage and traumatize children, as least why it did for me. Everyday I question whether my mother is actually my biological mother or not. I can't believe that I could be her son. She is so awful yet my father is so good. I have no doubts about my father whether he is my biological father or not but I do about my mother. I did not write this to describe how tiger mothers are bad and how Chinese mothers abuse their children. I wrote this story to tell you how one particular "Tiger mother" took things too far. As a result she lost her son, me. I can never respect my mother even if she paid me. I don't care if she has money, I can make my own. If I ever become successful, my mother will get food, shelter, and a monthly clothing allowance. Maybe medical insurance. But that's it. I do not wish to contact with her or even talk to her. This is the result of one tiger mother's fate. In essence she fucked up big time. I have no disdain for Chinese people, or for those who raise their children in a disciplined manner. I respect that. But its not for me. However I would suggest that parents learn from this and not repeat what my mother did. What I mean is how she treats other people as she treats me. Even for children in my opinion that is a fucked up way to raise them. They'll probably just end up hating their parents. Maybe. I will tell you though in my case, I lost respect for my mother. Even if she had done many good things for me, which I will admit she did, I still don't appreciate her because I don't like her principles.

It took me nearly seven hours to write this story. Maybe the years of forced English lessons without sleep by my mother finally paid off here. So that's my story. It was not written to be anything other than a perspective of a man. Specifically my perspective and how I viewed this tiger mother mentality. One might say that I reject this attitude with the same intensity as a tiger mother would encroach such strict values onto her children. It is a defense mechanism to counteract the feelings of insanity that I feel that I may otherwise incur. As of now I am still living with Joe and his family. I have also been diagnosed with Asperger's syndrome. I am not sure if that had impacted my life but that's what the psychologists say about me anyhow. I don't know what the future will bring onto me. Will I ever find love? Am I going to go crazy? Will I escape from the clutches of my mother? More importantly, will I ever be happy? These are questions that I can not answer. I have no idea what will happen to me. I can only wait to find out. Though I must say things are starting to get better from when I was younger. From this story, maybe you will get some insight about how one particular Chinese person thinks. The next time you see an Asian maybe you should take into consideration the suffering, abuse, and torture that it took them to be successful. After all, who wouldn't be better prepared for life after being forced to do things at such an early age, it is only natural that the individual should come out of it with some advantages. They will appreciate you for this consideration and you might be able to see why Asians are the way they are. Of course not all of them are stereotypically like this, after all it depends on the input to make the result. You would be surprised at their reaction. I think that some of them will be pleasantly surprised at your understanding. Others might be reminded of trauma. Still others, may not have had such a childhood. I was surprised when I asked people during my travels in China about this. To say the least they were amused. They had never fathomed that this upbringing might be detrimental to one's mental health. Then again, that was just the ones that I met. It will depend on the Asian you ask. No two people are the same. There might even be families of other races that raise their children in a similar manner. You ought to try it out sometime. I have one thing to say about all this and my suffering. If there is one thing that my suffering can be indicative of, this is it. If you are being treated like the way I was treated by my mother, don't take that shit. Stand up against it. CHALLENGE IT. No human being deserves to be treated like that. I really mean NO human being.

CPSIA information can be obtained at www.ICGtesting.com
Printed in the USA
236517LV00006B/83/P

9 780578 078939